Mimi Khalvati was born in Tehran, Iran, and grew up in England. She has published seven collections with Carcanet Press, including *The Meanest Flower*, shortlisted for the 2007 T.S. Eliot Prize, and *Child: New and Selected Poems 1991–2011,* a Poetry Book Society Special Commendation. In 2013 Smith/Doorstop Books published her pamphlet *Earthshine*, which was a Poetry Book Society Pamphlet Choice. She is the founder of the Poetry School, where she teaches. Her awards include a Cholmondeley Award from the Society of Authors and a major Arts Council Writer's Award. She is a Fellow of the Royal Society of Literature and of the English Society.

Also by Mimi Khalvati from Carcanet Press

MIMI KHALVATI

The Weather Wheel

CARCANET

First published in Great Britain in 2014 by
Carcanet Press Limited
Alliance House
Cross Street
Manchester M2 7AQ

www.carcanet.co.uk

A CIP catalogue record for this book is available from the British Library

ISBN 978 1 84777 258 9

The publisher acknowledges financial assistance from Arts Council England

Typeset by XL Publishing Services, Exmouth
Printed and bound in England by SRP Ltd, Exeter

Acknowledgements

Grateful thanks are due to the editors of the following publications in which some of these poems, or earlier versions of them, have appeared:

Acumen, Ariadne's Thread, Artemis, Cimarron Review (USA), *Genius Floored: Alphabet of Days* (Soaring Penguin Press, 2012), *Genius Floored: Uncurtained Window* (Soaring Penguin Press, 2013), *Her Wings of Glass* (Second Light Publications, 2014), *London Magazine, Magma, New Humanist, Not Only the Dark* (Categorical Books, 2011), *PN Review, POEM, Poetry London, Poetry Review, Poetry Salzburg Review, Taos Journal of International Poetry & Art* (www.taosjournalofpoetry.com), *The Book of Love and Loss* (Belgrave Press, Bath, 2014), *The Critical Muslim, The Editor: An Anthology for Patricia Oxley* (Rockingham Press, 2011), *The Forward Book of Poetry 2013, The Long Poem Magazine, The North, The Rialto, Tokens for the Foundlings* (Seren, 2012), *Urthona*.

'Model for a Timeless Garden' was commissioned by the Southbank Centre and written in response to Olafur Eliasson's eponymous light installation exhibited at the *Light Show*, Hayward Gallery, 2013.

'Ghazal: In Silence' appeared on the Academy of American Poets' website, Poem-a-Day.

Warm thanks to Peter and Ann Sansom for publishing *Earthshine* (Smith/Doorstop Books, 2013), a Poetry Book Society Pamphlet Choice. All the pamphlet poems are reproduced here.

I would also like to thank Martin Parker at Silbercow for designing the cover image, Alfred Corn, Jane Duran, Marilyn Hacker and Aamer Hussein for their generosity in reading and responding to the manuscript, and, in particular, Michael Schmidt and Helen Tookey for their invaluable editing.

Contents

VI   The Avenue

I Earthshine

House Mouse

Even the mist was daffodil yellow in the morning sun,
a slant of April sun that glowed on my banana skin.

And in the shadow of my arm a mouse lay, white belly up
like a lemur sunbathing. Begging she was, paws curled,

miniature paws like nail clippings, hind legs crossed
in a rather elegant fashion, tail a lollipop stick.

Pricked on her shadow, her ear and fur stood sharp as grass
but her real ear was soft, thin, pliable, faint as a sweetpea petal

and her shut eye a tiny arc like the hilum of a broad bean.
Yesterday she was plump. Today she's thin. Sit her up, she'll sit.

You can see how Lennie would have 'broke' his, petting it —
mine weighs no more than a hairball, nestling in my palm

as though it were wood pulp, crawlspace, a 'wee-bit housie'
and she, the pup, the living thing. The baby look's still on her.

And the depth of her sleep. I tuck her into the finger
of my banana skin — a ferryboat to carry her over the Styx.

Madame Berthe's Mouse Lemur

We should have been lemurs, lowering our metabolism
to suit, going into torpor in the cool dry winter months

to save on water and energy. We too should have sailed
on a raft of matted leaves out of poor Africa, out to Madagascar

into a forest of mangrove and thorn scrub, feeding off gum,
honeydew larvae, bedding down in tree holes *en famille.*

The very smallest of us, the veriest Tom Thumb, the most
minute pygmy, *tsitsidy, mausmaki,* itsy bitsy portmanteau,

little living furry torch, eyes two headlamp luminaries, front
a bib of chamois, tip to tail – and mostly tail – barely as long

as the line I write in, despite illegal logging, slash and burn,
would survive longer than many folk, especially in captivity.

Only the barn owl, goshawk, to watch for in the dark – raptors
with their own big beauty. But Madame Berthe's Mouse Lemur

is caught in the act – a chameleon clasped in her hands,
a geisha lowering her fan: the smallest primate on our planet.

Sun Sparrow

Sun, like a sparrow in the house, seeks dustgrounds
small as a handkerchief to play in. Sun sparrow, house sparrow,

I give you landing strips of dust on wood, runways
between photo frames, wood grain and wood knot roses,

nests of cane and cloth for you to steal, netherlands I never clean
for you to bathe in. Here's a dust bath, look, under the bed,

large enough for you and all your family. Why, even
the numbered hairs of my head, fallen, have lined a nest,

innumerable nests and silver they are, the better for you
to shine in. Come, sun, roost. And here is my skin. Warm it.

Sun sparrow, didn't Sappho herself have sparrows,
fair fleet sparrows, draw Aphrodite's chariot to wing her plea?

I ask no such thing. But I see you land, on wood, on wall,
take flight again and you who have your own warmth,

who need no streetlight, neon sign to roost in – why flee?
Be sociable, stay awhile on my flaking sill, hop right in.

Knifefish

Lit, lit, lit, lit are the estates at dawn:
honeycomb stairwells, corridors, landing lights,

flare paths for passengers flying home.
Three jets like electric fish streak the sky with rose.

Black ghost, ghost knifefish, how many days
since you went abroad, lurking in your murky pools,

locating dawn by sonar, by electric fields alone?
To image your world in darkness – driftwood

casting distortion shadows – no matter how weak
your receptor organ, faint its discharge, barely a volt,

through tail-bend, waveform, you fire, you feel,
sensing lightning, earthquake, your own kind

turning their dimmer switch up and down,
for this is how you talk. Old Aba Aba, grandpa,

with your one room lit at a time, feeling for walls,
navigating as surely as in the brightest, highest dawn!

Snail

Close the trapdoor. Let no light in. No,
not the luminous apricot cloud or whale cloud,

fat peach cloud or the isthmus of blue,
the sky lanes in between. Close the chink.

Sea slug, land snail, one head and one foot,
draw the one foot in. You are all head now,

helmet, foetus and dome, oceans under,
trapdoor sealed. Safe, safe, safe.

Snail-deep, slug-dark, shu-shu-shush.
Waves roll in. But here you are landed,

relic on the sand. The moon has carried you
on his back but what do you know of love?

Its arrow, smear of silk. And of hatred?
Salt, drawing your love juice into its grains,

giving you age, old age and its snail-slow shrivelling.
Be lazy, snail, be slow. Savour every inch.

Sciurus Carolinensis

Sun rivers on glass, threatens to mount, blaze
into my eyeline so that, heat-struck, I headlong

down to hump squirrelled in the shade below, leaves
moving as I move, as grass moves with the snake.

I am the grey. Born helpless, blind and deaf.
My mother lays me across her forepaws, fetches me

out of a cave, weans me once my teeth appear.
Sciurus names only my *skia*, shadow, *oura*, tail.

I displace the red. Acorn-bred, carrier of the pox,
I infect it with lesions, ulcers, scabs, weeping crusts,

it shivers, shivers, *skia*, *oura*, and then it's dead.
I mean no harm. I'm no image seared on your brain

only seen side on, tail up, ears tufted like conifer spurs;
no nutkin on a branch, jug on a wall, graphic loop,

no ampersand between presentiment and trace.
Skia, *oura*, I flicker on the walls of the cave.

The Conservatory

If you keep two blinds down and one blind up
and sit under the one that's up under the skylight

and the Sunday morning rain, you create –
at absolutely no expense – the kind of conservatory

you've always wanted but without the wicker
and kelims, the view onto the dripping garden

and the cat, all soaking, hidden under a hedge.
You are elevated instead. You are a bird in a nest.

Rick as a small boy sold birds for pocket money.
He made his own trap out of a wire washing basket,

a stick, some fishing line, some bread, catching
sparrows, dunnocks and, if he was lucky, a finch,

before progressing to proper trap cages with a call bird
that would sing and attract more birds he'd extricate,

sell, then start over again. Now he's a mouse-catcher
with no pension. 'You're not illegible', he said they said.

The Little Gloster

With such icy winds, facing the rising sun in the garden
makes no difference so I take shelter on the terrace,

comforted by two black sheepskins, one under me,
one over, kindly provided by the establishment.

Seagulls, seen from below, their red feet neatly stowed,
beaks and eyes painted like wooden toys, hang

immobile long enough to be scrutinised in flight
before they swerve away. Propped against a fence,

a reindeer is spotted with fairy lights you expect to see
vanish like daylight stars and everything that loomed

last night on a smuggler's night black with storm
– the distillation tower's disembodied four red eyes –

retreats into its rightful place. Young waiters, chefs,
preparing for the fair, are lining up white deckchairs

close enough to the seafront to feel spray. Sandwiched
in these sheepskins, I am half man, half sheep, myself.

Microchiroptera

Only human noises populate the night. No owl, pheasant,
wailing fox, only stars that have buried their heads in cloud.

Listening becomes a momentous task. The eye as always
fights for supremacy and the ear, fazed as a bat in rain,

imagining it hears a rush of water, hears 'all things hushed'.
O *chauve-souris*, flying mouse, leather mouse, flittermouse,

jealous naked microbat, winged seed of sycamore,
umbrella man, acrobat hanging in your own skin parachute,

flying patagium carpet, O bat-being in fairy wings,
string purse, anus face, where are your echoes now

– dry flutter of a mothwing, rustle of a centipede –
where is your pulsing cry, your lovesong in the dark?

In the vast homelessness of a country night – dear country,
left behind – we come back into our moral being, back

into the animal ground of our being under the absent stars.
Under their roofs and rafters, we navigate that ground.

The Landing Stage

How slippery the path just at the end where the indigo stutters
of dragonflies rain against glass water! Where everything is flower –

the air, its scent, cabbage whites, single, paired; pines, cedars,
carpet dew; where old age flowers in its slow walk to the water;

where the left brain flowers and the right, the lawnmower
sprays grass fountains; where sadness settles for the pine cones,

not knowing if they are really pine cones at this distance;
where Anne flowers in an orange shawl and our lungs

are grey wildflowers, minds a mindless garden; where,
in the event of fire, we are to collect at the bottom of the lawn.

We are to collect our belongings, blankets, iPads, medicines.
We are to collect sunlight silvering on our shoulders.

Our shoulders are thin. We collect our thinness, our boniness,
in a huddle of silver water down by the river. Be careful!

they warn me, those who are, going down to the landing stage
raised high enough to dangle younger legs over the water.

Earthshine

Under the giant planes beside the gate where we said goodbye,
the one bare trunk where squirrels flatten themselves on bark

side by side with a voluminous plane whose ivy outraces branch,
under the two great planes where we stood vaguely looking round

since it was a clear night, the street empty and we, small gaggle,
newly intimate but standing a yard apart, keeping our voices low

though they carried bright as bells as we counted the evening out,
gestured towards the cars, deciding who would go with whom

and gradually splitting off, under the planes with the squirrel dreys
hidden in all that ivy, but hanging low directly above the station,

there, where we looked pointing, like an Oriental illustration
of Arabian Nights, lay the old moon in the new moon's arms:

earthshine on the moon's night side, on the moon's dark limb,
earthlight, our light, our gift to the moon reflected back to us.

And the duty we owe our elders as the Romans owed their gods
– duties they called pietàs, we call pity – shone in the moon's pietà.

Prunus Avium

We buried my mother's ashes in the holes, the four
we dug to plant four cherry trees for her, *Prunus avium*:

wild cherry, sweet cherry, bird cherry, gean or mazzard,
each name carrying something of *Prunus avium* on the wind,

the wind that blew drifts of ash like bonemeal across clay.
In three years they'll be grown; in twenty, diamond woodland.

But we'll recognise our trees, set back where the path ends.
Surrounding them will be native oak, beech, alder, hazel.

One cherry tree from each of us: Tara, Bea, Kai and myself.
And on Tom's behalf, we invoked the name of Yax Tum Bak,

Mayan God of Planting, there in a desolate, bitterly windy field
in Buckinghamshire. Clay stuck to our boots in grassy clumps

and as Tara heaved her spade, worms, lustrous as white mulberries,
fled, upturned. Later, in the Garden Centre – 'Oh, how beautiful!'

my mother would have gasped on entering – I bought Tara
a peach tree for Valentine's Day, *Prunus persica*, from Persia.

II   Under the Vine

Under the Vine

Yes, I should be living under the vine,
dapple at my feet and the bare dry dust

singing of drought, of heat. Look at the pile
of rubble round the roots, curled dried leaves,

mound of ant homes I can't see. Look at
the flower fallen in the dirt, flake yellow,

listen to the wasps, the bees. And the vine
above me, the vine that smells of nothing,

yields nothing but the music of its name,
the memory of some long-forgotten terrace.

Yes, under a flock of swallows that repeat
– because we have to believe it – the end,

the end, nearly the end of a summer
so long it knows neither month nor week.

Yes, I should keep my happiness hidden,
under the vine, from those who envy it.

Starlight

Only the brightest stars were out with a half moon
centred in the sky: a ceiling to learn the names of stars by.

And in the gaps between the stars, milkcarts went to market,
pony traps crossed viaducts, oxen drove sad water-wheels,

history trundled by as birds awoke and the distant sound
of a plane winked lights. Her owl flew back to Minerva

as she flashed her shield while, on Apadana's stairways,
processions of bearded guards, Persians, Medes, marched past.

Cedar palaces were torched; frigates, night-fishing boats set out.
Passengers flew like vesper bats straight across the moon,

roofscapes listened for child lovers leaning over balconies,
geraniums grew in the dark. I had never been so happy

and historical. Happy enough to see, holding them up,
stars on the tip of each finger, countable, spread far apart,

one by one go out as day rose to pluck the first strains
of a Spanish guitar. Then the silver moon went white.

Angels

Updraughts lift sounds of language imperceptibly, even
the silent language of Lula as she hobbles up the steps.

Dogs Lula doesn't know bark along the terraces, cockerels,
though it isn't dawn, crow anyway. It could be any village

anywhere in the world, everything in decay. But things
retain their scent – the rubbed tomato leaf – and sound

– the bamboo river – and as if heard behind closed doors,
the angels: angel of September, of the fallen fig and dapple;

angel of perspective that staggers the terraces upward,
white steps downward; angels of the sister mountains –

the first, the second, the third. And the angels, cowled,
circle us like lepers on the hills, they unveil themselves.

And I love my angels not as they were in childhood,
angel of the crab-apple and chine, of calico and sandal,

but as they are: leprous and discharged, violent and betrayed.
Angel of the soft wind that blows across my breasts.

Orchard

However small, it's still an orchard –
three limes, a pomegranate and a kumquat.

Each stands in a circle of shade
and bedding plants. Sweetpeas brought

from England have died at the foot
of their canes. Above, the pepper tree

that went wild in a sudden storm,
throwing its branches all over the place,

hangs droops of coral berries against
a calendar sky. Cones, black droppings

in the dust, a fragment of rope
knotted at both ends, a fleeting shadow –

a swallow if you look up. But no,
I keep my gaze on the ground.

If the trees were horses, they'd be foals
and the pepper tree their barn.

What it Was

It was the pool and the blue umbrellas,
blue awning. It was the blue and white

lifesize chess set on the terrace, wall of jasmine.
It was the persimmon and palm side by side

like two wise prophets and the view that dipped
then rose, the swallows that turned the valley.

It was the machinery of the old olive press,
the silences and the voices in them calling.

It was the water talking. It was the woman
reading with her head propped, wearing glasses,

the logpile under the overhanging staircase,
mist and the mountains we took for granted.

It was the blue-humped hose and living wasps
swimming on the surface. It was the chimneys.

It was sleep. It was not having a mother,
neither father nor mother to comfort me.

Marrakesh I

On our last day on the roof terrace, our own 'heavenly message
of the third floor' that Matisse had in mind for *Les Marocains*,

the air's so still not even the cellophane of my cigarette packet
blows out of the ashtray. Morning sun lies on me like a blanket,

le baromètre a remonté d'un quart de cadran while down in the storeroom,
where two caged budgerigars have never seen the light of day,

il fait clair comme dans une cave. Daisy, the indoor cat, grubs around
the soil of the young olive where a few wild grasses in the tub

are all she will ever know of lawns. Fatiha has watered the palm,
oleander, succulents and a dribble of water crossing a barrier

of sun and shade gleams like oil. The cat moves soundlessly,
the sun with stealth until the shade, the chill, swallows our feet.

There's no accounting for joy, the way it bubbles in the most arid
of deserts or rains blue gold. The muezzin climbs the minaret

in leather mules not on foot but by donkey as if riding, hill by hill,
into Jerusalem. Proust's voice obeys the laws of night and honey.

Marrakesh II

I have been looking for the famous gentleness of light
floating on the paper field in the pink city and have seen it

only in passing: as we crept into the old town, the taxi
nudging the cyclists, donkey carts, through mud-walled lanes

as if entering a bible story; in the smoky vaporous haze,
the smoky hooded figures enveloped by it, each man a Yeats

declaring 'I am a crowd, I am a lonely man, I am nothing';
in the blind walled pink of the Tombeaux Saâdiens at sunset,

set off by small red rosebeds, a tall magenta bougainvillea,
the colours proceeding by pulsation, exhaled from within;

seen it in the mosaic of light falling through the reed roof
in the Berber souk or down thin alleys of keyhole arches.

Travelling on a paddleboat to Corazón, battling a channel
of reeds and branches, Paul Bowles wrote that it was like

being in the bloodstream of a giant and so it is, immersed
in a memory of sundown, at any hour, in all his arteries.

Marrakesh III

To see him at his easel, *H. Matisse par lui-même*, black hat,
tailcoat, beard, glasses, on a camp stool facing a marabout

in pen and ink is to feel a small breeze coming off the pages.
A horseman, acanthus, basket of oranges, a smoker at the window,

another, another, the medina, the portal of the Casbah mosque,
Seated Moroccan, Standing Moroccan, a calla lily and bindweed,

riffle like water through my palms while I sit surrounded,
three floors up, by the same raised, lowered, false perspectives.

But Arcadia is not something to project into deep space
but onto the surface of memory. *Ah! que le monde est grand*

à la clarté des lampes! Aux yeux du souvenir que le monde est petit!
In Jemaa El Fna, the lanterns are lit. They congregate like stars,

tin palaces of fire and flame, a sultanate of miniature cities.
But at cruising altitude, above streaks of indigo and purple clouds,

a blood continent broods on black estuaries, archipelagos, reefs,
for black is the simplifying force of memory. It is a form of elegy.

Marrakesh IV

'These recumbent figures, all in the same gray nuance,
such a soothing gray, whose faces are represented by

a yellow-ocher oval, you know that they were not always
painted like that. Look! At the top, the man on the left,

he was red! The other, next to him, was blue; the other
was yellow. Their faces had lines, eyes, a mouth.

The one at the top smoked a pipe... The slippers, the pipe,
the lines of the face, the varied color of the burnooses,

why have they all melted away?' *C'est que je vais*
vers mon sentiment; vers l'extase... et puis, j'y trouve le calme.

J'ai mon bol de poissons et ma fleur rose. C'est ce qui m'avait frappé!
ces grands diables qui restent des heures, contemplatifs, devant

une fleur et des poissons rouges. Eh bien! Si je les fais rouges,
ce vermillon va rendre ma fleur violette! Alors? je la veux rose,

ma fleur! autrement elle n'est plus! Au lieu que mes poissons,
ils pourraient être jaunes, cela ne me fait rien: ils seront jaunes!

Marrakesh V

The floral motif is the initial cell from which the pattern
spreads to the edges of the cloth, canvas, the material world

which is drained of meaning and hierarchy. In its place
the underlying void, aerated, animated, expands like gas

until cloth, rug, garden, agave, succulents, yukka, cacti
and sky-high bamboo forest revert to dreamlike pentimenti.

Jemaa El Fna, once a bus station, has been recognised as
a Masterpiece of the Oral and Intangible Heritage of Humanity

but Berber water-sellers, snake-charmers, storytellers, scribes,
shoeblacks, tooth-pullers, mendicants, fortune-tellers, masseurs,

are more than oral, intangible, in a plaza where no building
should rise higher than a palm tree. Near the Koutoubia,

the booksellers' mosque, Lalla Zohra, the children's saint,
entombed in a castellated, icing-white cube, makes her escape

and visits us regularly. A woman by day, a dove by night,
she sits against the skyline silently, as if transfixed by chanting.

Marrakesh VI

More megaphone than bird, his whole body pulsing,
the Sahari House Bunting, stringing himself along

the riad's parapet, repeats himself ad infinitum
with a second's pause to catch breath. In that pause,

his mate replies but with a different call, a yes, maybe,
or occasionally interrupts without disturbing his rhythm.

On his ledge, he rotates to the north, south, east, west,
calling out to the four corners of Marrakesh while she,

catching the sun in flight, fans this way and that before
flitting back to her perch. Now he's on the corner outpost

of his sentry walk, faithfully plugging away and finally
stunned into silence as the braying starts – a most marvellous

cacophony of muezzins from Ben Youssef, Sidi Ishak,
Mouassine, Ben Salah, Koutoubia, Berrima, crowning noon

until, with a lone *Allahu Akba-a-r*, the last muezzin's *adhan*,
melting distance into song and song into the distance, dies away.

Le Café Marocain

This is the soul. In aqua and gold.
It rhymes with the body as burquas do,

as birdsong with arches, nine to a wall.
The goldfish are spoonfuls of honey,

spoonfuls that dissolve in the bowl.
Glass is the ground of contemplation,

this and a flower, the three-pronged rose.
The gold of men's calves, feet, hands

– lower limbs the body in broadcloth
set loose as it burned off in smoke –

was the first idea, as the soul is, before
the image, the afterthought was formed.

This is the last we shall see of the fathers
in grey burnooses, meadowsweet turbans,

faceless in ovals, forgetful in youth:
this ore, this residue in the alchemical bowl.

III The Soul Travels on Horseback

New Year's Eve

Night is a rush of noise, an Indian hilltown train
steaming up gradients through Himalayan tunnels,

morning the destination, quiet as a mountain top
after the snow has melted, celebrants have left:

a Shimla of the mind, its local aspirations – work,
money, kinship, health; a time to think things over,

let them settle in the recesses of imagination.
They'll raise their heads of their own accord, lean

out of carriages to wave. For now is the time
of watering the splendid platform displays, of

gathering at The Ridge, the Scandal Point in the mall,
fingering oak and rosewood souvenirs. In Shimla,

mashkis will be carrying goatskin bags of water,
sluicing down the tarmac while I, at the last

hill station of the year, will bring the silence in,
fold it like a three-flower Kullu shawl on my table.

The Pear Tree

And when there's no poetry in it, the hour, the sky,
only cumulus and the first faint ossicles of rain

pattering on glass like a bone bundle thrown
for a shaman to divine, when no answer comes,

faith gives up, brain slackens, skin sloughs off
like a turtle shedding old scutes from its shell,

when the same dread incubus squats on the heart,
hiding a breathing hole on the top of his head

for all breath, desire, have long fled his mouth,
when friends disappear – and were they friends? –

and your head on its single stem weighed down
heavy as a baby pear tree not with pome or pear

but with time's three globes, what then,
little pear tree, bletted by frost? A rootstock

has dwarfed you the better to bear but quince,
pear, whose bridal kiss will you perfume now?

Rain Stories

Huddling under an umbrella like two old lovers
arm in arm under the pouring rain, we took up

where we had left off, catching up on the years,
their stories common knowledge now – rain

audible and visible. (Affection returned though
before we share such rain it will be years again.)

But mine at home, and only mine, is secretive,
soundless and so fine, it's only against darker leaves

it reveals itself. Winter, it tells me, means
'the time of water'; raindrops, it shows me,

are spheres and only tear-shaped when they fall –
though in Oaxaca the Church of Santa Teresita

had a glorious rain of roses; more instances,
it gives me, from its own backstory as in –

a r. of kisses, 1893, of calm moonbeams, 1821,
melody, 1820, frogs, 1593, of sparks, tears, 1541.

Aunt Moon

Aunt Moon, Old Glamour Moon in a haze of smoke
puffing behind your folding screen, Old Barren Moon

with your round pig belly, what lies, what lies!
I love you for the lies you've told! Lies with a belly

of milk, lies to call the children in, gather them
round your mirror fogged, Old Moon, with death.

No lying now, is there? No creeping round the houses,
sly Jokester Moon with your pearly teeth, implants

that went wrong, aren't they? One look at the truth
and you vanish. O what a clear clear sky, clear as day!

But I saw you, Moon, in the doorway. Spliced in two
as the glass revolved, in purdah with your back turned.

Who were you whispering to, Aunt Moon? No one,
was there? No one ever to lisp to, bribe, stab in the back,

no one to avenge. No, the best lies are told with a bevy
of innocent stars in your eyes, not in a revolution's doorway.

Statham Grove Surgery

Seen in disbelief through fug in the workmen's caff
with its canisters of snow, in the panoramic distance

of Clissold Park wearing its hood of grey wool, chef's hat
in the snow, behind a fallen tree trunk languid as a nude,

a human hare, grey on grey, white gloves, white hind paws,
is shadowboxing while their trainer, red on grey, holds up

focus mitts for a second sparring jackrabbit, black on grey,
like the hare on the moon. Amber eyes glide down the road;

horse chestnuts waltz in whalebone, braceletted with crows;
my cappuccino breathes out smoke. Ruled on park railings,

black is a marriage of scissors and snow. But in Statham Grove,
among red pillar-box hills, gold corridor woods, we turn into

house plants, umbrella plants, gum trees, rubber leaf hands
still charged with snow, deaf to a story a young dragon tree

hears, enthralled. Dr West wears a bright red stethoscope.
Homeward bound, we leave footprints in a black leaf fall.

The Wardrobe

How secluded we are under a sun we should be out in.
Cupboarded in shadow, one foot in twilight, we tilt.

Childhood snuffs its master light, light we need to love
and be loved by, to write, to read. Else all is dusk,

dusk in the heart, in all our finer feelings. Had I
a wardrobe of my mother's furs, mink, fox, Persian lamb,

how my heart would sink. I'd slide my fingers along the rail,
feel the carcass weight of coats, shoulders zipped in plastic,

how the metal hook of the hanger sticks, see the bridge,
German bridge, where I wore my own grey astrakhan,

a yellow patch of impetigo on my chin. A dirty disease.
From masturbation, unclean hands, some kind of lonely shit.

It has to be foetal or under three days old, a Karakul lamb,
barely able to stand on the kill floor where dozens more

are bleating, or its pelt will lose colour, curl, lustre,
and its meat is simply tossed, too meagre even to eat.

Fog

World is headless, cut off at the waist and we, bundled,
seeing snowflakes only as they pass across a face,

we earth dwellers who know heaven's a cloud, a bank,
an upperwhere, otherwhere, whose cloud deck homes

lure our spirits with lights in the fog, paraffin stoves,
our Bethlehems, our backyards become Bethlehems,

we whose hearts race the blinder we grow, we moles,
we dirt-tossers, we mouldywarps with no eyes or ears

with a mouth at one end, anus at the other, we pipes,
we cylinders, who have stockpiled our subterranean hell,

our mole runs, underground galleries, larders for a clew
of earthworms, we labour of moles with paws like rakes –

what have we left but these hands now, we boars, we sows
with four limbs, one nose, a body plan and a taupe pelt?

World is headless and we, who have only touch and smell,
must touch and smell gas, smoke bombs, blood meal, bait.

Snow is

Snow is a rubbing of sorts, a wax heelball on ground,
an impress of ribs – exoskeletons in high and low relief.

Each snowflake is witness to the cloud-womb that formed it,
how wet, how warm, the union of crystals, how powdery.

Trapped in firn, air will evidence ash from Krakatoa,
deposits from lead smelters, pollen and greenhouse gases.

Snow is adjectival. On foliage particularly, discriminates
between the feathery and lobed, the linear and pointilliste.

In itself is silent, but on contact, creaks. Acquires an air
of sanctity in repose but in action earns oaths and profanities.

Snow is a friend to children, those who have scarves, mittens,
snowboards and wooden sledges. To others, it is the devil's own,

akin to the djinn who frequent sinkholes, wherever mud rejoices.
To the children housed in sheep sheds, chicken coops, tents,

dressed in cut-up blankets, seeing things that aren't there in forests,
snow is the devil they know. Better him than the live bombing.

The Blanket

Cold, yes, under a sodium sky at three o'clock in the morning.
But there's this shawl to wear and tea with Manuka honey

and across the only gap in the border, a thousand refugees an hour
pouring through Ras al-Jedir. An hour? By morning, my morning,

another five thousand, by lunchtime, another five and how many
have even a striped hemp blanket? Fifteen thousand blankets!

Imagine one. The way it folds stiffly as a tent around the head
bent back, the shoulders jutting, knees drawn up, wrists free,

the lone triangular edifice. Feel the weave. Hairy, ridged.
Smell it. Determine the sightlines either side of the hollowed cheeks.

Imagine the scene in silence, not as it would be. The blanket
as a block, a wood carving. The tools: straight gouge, spoon gouge,

back bent, dog leg, fishtail chisels, V-tools, punches, vices;
hook knives, drawknives, rasps and rifflers, mallets, saws, abrasives;

slip waterstones – how quiet they sound – and strops for sharpening.
Figure in a blanket. In acacia, sycamore or, most likely, olive.

The Swarm

Snow was literally swarming round the streetlamp like gnats.
The closer they came, the larger they grew, snow gnats, snow bees,

and in my snood, smoking in the snow, I watched them.
Everyone else was behind the door, I could hear their noise

which made the snow, the swarm, more silent. More welcome.
I could have watched for hours and seen nothing more than specks

against the light interrupting light and away from it, flying blind
but carrying light, specks becoming atoms. They flew too fast

to become snow itself, flying in a random panic, looming close
but disappearing, like flakes on the tongue, at the point of recognition.

They died as they landed, riding on their own melting as poems do
and in the morning there was nothing to be seen of them.

Instead, a streak of lemon, lemon honey, rimmed the sky
but the cloud lid never lifted, the weekend promised a blizzard.

I could have watched for hours and seen nothing more than I do now,
an image, metaphor, but not the blind imperative that drove them.

Model for a Timeless Garden

You are the shadows who have miniaturised the cryosphere
into a garden of paradise, yours the silhouettes facing fire.

Yours the skeletons, crystal wasps in the long black coffin,
spiders with egg sacs and glass intestines, stalagmites, goblins,

vertebrae and antlers, melting candles, yours the serpents
swallowing mice; infinite, interminable, your Lazarus dance.

Have you seen aerial fossils, spiculae, birdwings frozen in flight?
Kittens iced to branches, glazed drops, objects crystallised by light?

Yours the glass apple, glass core, that ballooning missing bite;
the wedding arch of crossed swords, apertures jagged as kites.

Go home and imagine them, you can't. Even as they're here,
now, they're gone. And everything outdoors, buildings by the river,

boats, buses on the bridge, everything that runs in lines will run
into fountain, the beauty of the arc against the formality of line.

Yours this catwalk, ghastly, spectacular, and all the faery forms
of fungus, plankton, Venus's girdle, that have swum through time.

The Soul Travels on Horseback

and the road is beset with obstacles and thorns.
But let it take its time for I have hours and hours to wait

here, snowbound in Lisbon, glad of this sunlit café
outside Departures, for an evening flight to Heathrow.

Being my soul's steed, I should like to know its name
and breed – a Marwari of India, Barb of North Africa,

the Akhal-Teke of Western Asia or a Turkoman,
now extinct? Is it the burnt chestnut colour of the ant,

grey as a Bedouin wind, the four winds that made it?
O Drinker of the Wind, I travel by air, sea, land

and wherever I am, there you are behind my back
pounding the cloud streets, trailing banners of cirrus

or as Platero once did, from fear or chill, hoofing a stream,
breaking the moon into a swarm of clear, crystal roses.

No, no matter your thirst, ride swiftly, mare, stallion,
mother, father, for without you I feel forever homesick.

IV Tears

The Overmind

Even when I was a child, tears were something
other children had – a permission I didn't understand

other people gave, I thought the children gave it
to themselves: a special treat when they'd already

had their share. My overmind, as H.D. called it,
isn't a jellyfish, a kind of swimming cap on my head.

My overmind seems to be this sadness – I nearly always
carry it and it *is* a kind of hat, skysize, skyshape.

I feel sorry for my smallness, short trunk, short legs,
sleeves rolled up, feet too large to be in proportion.

When I sit and plant them squarely, side by side like shoes
with no one in them, I feel how flat they are and firm.

If I were a pot, a round ceramic pot with a mustard glaze
on a whatnot in the guest room or on an outside table,

I'd be, like H.D.'s Delphic charioteer whose feet made
'a firm pedestal for himself', I'd be always balanced.

Reading the Saturday Guardian

A yellow ladybird is reading the *Guardian Weekend*,
alternately reading and grooming, rubbing her hands,

slapping the sides of her face. To do so, she tilts back
on her tail, rearing up as if into a magnifying mirror.

For the time being, she's entirely forgotten about flight –
the ridgy terrain of a brown paper bag, a valley dotted

with croissant lakes, is only a ten-minute hike away.
Of course she isn't yellow yellow – more goldenrod

with many black spots, a black and white harlequin head.
I present her with a flake. Momentarily, she looks baffled,

rears again and, in the one instant I look away, disappears.
Next thing I know the ladybird and (croissant) flake –

twice her size – have toppled over the rim of the *Guardian*,
one on top of the other – a perfect landing, ladybird on flake

like man in boat, then, capsizing out of sight, she sails
over the edge of the table, the table travelling to Portslade.

Midsummer Solstice

Sun keeps taking its jacket off and putting it on again.
So, down here, do I. Of every shape and size and species,

wasps, flies, bees, midges, gnats, gather in this seeded
cottage garden like pilgrims to a church. The foxglove bud

hasn't yet unfurled, tug at it tug tug but there's no entry here.
So the blithe bee flies away. How busy skies once were

– as they are now – with a glut of nectar, colour, nestled
between rock walls to draw them in – fleets of giddy insects.

They land on my glasses, thigh, buzz around my hair,
whizz by, zoom in and out of vision but nothing annoys me

except my clumsy language, my laggard apprehensions.
Sleep, sleep is the only word I hear. I'd curl up in it

as a bee in a foxglove bell. And I see the blonde schoolboy
at Leeds station, left on a bench with a younger brother

and a punnet of raspberries to look after, calling out *Mum!*
holding a finger up in the air, capped with a raspberry bell.

Picking Raspberries with Mowgli

It was when he leant close to me, his little naked torso,
brown and thin, reaching an arm into the row of raspberries,

that I snatched a kiss. The raspberries smelled of rosemary
and among them, like a cuckoo's egg, grew the odd sweetpea.

Do you know why they're called sweetpeas? Mowgli asked.
No, why? Because look, he said, fingering a sick pale pod,

this is the fruit and this is the flower and inside the pod are peas.
Mowgli looked inside things. Inside the sieve, a spiderling

trailing a thread his finger trailed up, over, under the pile
of fruit he prodded. Don't pick the ones with the white bits,

Mowgli ordered, they taste horrid. Sun tangled in the canes,
cobwebs blurred the berries. Mowgli progressed to the apples –

small bitter windfalls. I'm going to test them, he said, for smashes.
Mowgli, throwing apples high against the wall – and missing;

Mowgli squinting, testing the poor things now for bruises; Mowgli
balancing on a rake, first thing in the morning, grinning shyly.

Sniff

It was Sniff who chose Kai, not the other way round, at Sharon's
Fugly Rats, by licking him all over, grooming him, virtually everything

short of saying *please choose me*. In the car, he sat quietly in his hand.
And now it's only Kai he comes to, sniffing, only Kai he's bonded with.

Sharon breeds dumbo rats, sometimes top-eared, rex and smooth
as well as hairless and double rex in a variety of colours and markings –

great pets, well handled, not 'the cowaring wrecks you can sometimes see'.
Sitting next to Kai on our deckchairs, I am finally introduced to Sniff

– 'feel his tail, it's really soft' – on my birthday. The size of him!
Sniff is a cinnamon hooded fancy rat, hooded not only by the fur

cinnamon saddle that runs the length of his spine but also, currently,
by Kai's t-shirt sleeve, whom I have presented – for his owner's birthday –

with a three-tiered rat cage complete with double hammock, straw nest,
swinging tunnel, mineral tube, cat litter tray and dog potty training pad.

I hope he knows who he is. To find out more, visit Fancy Rats Forum
whose menu includes bulletins, articles, reviews, tutorials and obituaries.

Drawing Bea

Her voice had that dreamy quality that made me think
she had been watching telly, so early on Sunday morning.

When it brightened as I said 'It's Granny Mimi', I did,
for a moment, feel like Granny Mimi as if she had brought me

slippers, a cup of coffee. 'What were you doing?' 'What?'
'Were you watching telly?' imagining her under a blanket,

curled on the sofa, slightly sulky. 'Mum's drawing me.'
'Drawing you?' 'Yes, Mum's doing a drawing of me.'

I saw the darkened room and, in a spotlight somewhere,
Bea keeping unbelievably still. I heard the stump of charcoal

hatching, shading, stroking her hair, her mother breathing;
felt her whole outline being transposed, lifted like a transparency.

But the reality was they were facing each other, like card players,
across the kitchen table. While Tara drew Bea, Bea drew Tara:

heads down, heads only, a shoulder, an arm maybe, no hands,
quick sketches on copy paper – Tara's to bin, Bea's to sort out later.

Nocturne

Parked cars are sleeping like animals in their baskets.
Sally, Bea's corn snake, coils by her rock and the mollies

who know neither night nor day keep swimming round
and round behind glass. Lucky the brain awash with sleep

flushing its toxins out. However, according to my mother,
so groggy in the mornings, she never slept a wink all night.

What did she do during those long useless hours? Worry,
endlessly worry, take more pills, eat something sweet, biskwits

as she called them, never more than one or two at a time?
The dead have taken our questions with them, leaving,

in their stead, fresh shocks: discoveries in drawers, files,
that become the significant things we remember them by:

not the memories that swim round and round behind glass
– how they were, how we knew them when they were alive –

but realisations after the fact, small sleepless leapings
and floodings, spasms, nocturnal poundings in the heart.

The Waves

Every day the world is beloved by me, the seagull eager
for its perch. I woke this morning to a darkened room,

my soul stabled at the gate. We grow older, quieter,
hearing degrees of movement, distance, and the dead

would listen if they could to the voices of the living
as bedrock listens to the ocean. I listen to the waves,

trying to make them go one, two, one, two, to hear
what Virginia Woolf heard. But she heard it in memory,

darling memory that delineates. One, two, one, two,
and all the variable intervals in between surrendering

to 'the very integer' Alice Oswald rhymed with water,
creating a thumb-hole through which to see the world.

Light fluctuates and my soul fluctuates like a jellyfish
underwater. My hand throws animal shadows on paper

and there, outlined, is a single goat, black and white,
standing on top of the mountain, like a tiny church.

Similes

The yacht lies like an elegant equation in the mind.
Last night it lay on black velvet like a glasswing butterfly,

wings folded, two tall masts. The straightness of the horizon
never ceases to be astonishing, putting one in a daze –

only a slight swell in the water to prove that we are not
in a painted vestibule, that this is not an annunciation.

And here's the yellow ferry which reminds me of
Elizabeth Bishop's desk; my table, metallic, sunflecked,

of Hockney's swimming pools. Everything is always
like something else. Each makes love to the other.

You are like me, they say. Blue paint has spattered
the whitewash, speckled the flagstones – the eye jumps

from blue to blue, island to island, raisin to raisin in a cake.
Archie hated raisins in cake, peas in rice. His beard

was salt and pepper, white at the time of death. To have
one terrible disease gives you no immunity against another.

Cherries and Grapes

He stood up in my dream, very tall, and said: Mum,
I've got — Syndrome. The missing word's a dream word,

a bottom-of-the-sea, a carried-on-the-wind word.
Being so tall, my son has eyes like fruit in a tree, glassy,

Rainier cherries very high up. One cannot reach them.
The worse the news, the further they recede on the branch.

Talking of Richard who had an epileptic fit this morning,
Giorgos, who has seen it all, with that warm faraway look

in his eyes, stands shaking his head, 'So young...'
while his father, still spry, turns aside, shaking out nets –

but what's the fishing like these days? No one says.
This is how the world is today. And this is how I am in it,

rising from a siesta. My granny would have brought me
grape juice, white *asgari* she had crushed and sieved herself

and I would have drunk it slowly, ruckling, then smoothing,
the green chenille at her table. This is how the world was then.

Kusa-Hibari

It was June and every barnacled brick of the sea wall
was drying out as we were. Had it been October,

had I been Hearn, I too would have kept a grass lark,
a Kusa-Hibari. Why? Not only because he sings,

not only because he is also called Autumn Wind,
Morning Bell, Little Bell of the Bamboo Grove,

or because he's worth more than his weight in gold,
being half the size of a barley grain, or even because

his antennae, longer than his body, are so very fine
they can only be seen when held against the light

as they will be held since to find him, you must turn
his cage round and round to discover his whereabouts,

but because, as his guardian tells me, his tiny song,
song of love and longing, 'is unconsciously retrospective:

he cries to the dust of the past – he calls to the silence
and the gods for the return of time' is why I'd want him.

Tears

In the first weeks after my mother's death,
I curled up like a foetus on the side of my heart.

My tears were like fresh water, warm and clear.
They flowed of their own accord, soundlessly,

while my body, my mouth and even my eyelids
lay as peacefully as in sleep and the more tears flowed,

the more I wanted them. World was foetal then.
But in the months that followed, tears dried up

and world took up its stick and walked blindly
through the riverbeds. Had they been floodplains,

had there been no dams to render them obsolete,
nilometers would have measured the overflow

from faraway monsoons on stairs, pillars, wells.
Too high and there'd be famine, too low, the same.

I measured distances by her. My mother my compass,
my almanac and sundial, drawing me arcs in space.

V   Her Anniversary

The Goat

The goat, the earliest known ruminant in the world
and hence, one might say, our first poet-philosopher,

is not ruminating now but, nose against purple plastic,
is dribbling a ball among pigeons. When he rears

against the wire fencing, towering above us, he displays,
dangling on his neck, his two wattles or toggles or tassles –

a dimorphic trait maybe, caruncles with no known function.
We cannot touch the goat or feed him. But children do,

they want to feel the fearful thrill of his tongue, his lips,
they want to console, thank him for being among us.

Does he miss his mountains? The properties of spheres
in motion are no compensation for limestone gorges,

healing dittany and sage. The pigeons peck peck peck.
The old buck ruminates. And a toddler stoops to grass,

tugs at a handful she thrusts into the air above her head
and lets fall on her father's shoes, like Newton's apple.

On the Occasion of his 150th Anniversary

Let's fling down a cloak of gold leaf on wove paper,
let's do the pavement like Klimt. Like his father

before him, Ernst Klimt the Elder, gold engraver,
and his brother who took up engraving later –

whose deaths in one year were the fount of his vision –
let's do acacia in a shower of coins, engrave each face

with *The Kiss*. Semen is flowing like golden rain,
double yellow lines meander in gold metallic ink

and the streetlamps are on – *O spark of the Gods!* –
it's snowing gold flake, sweeping mosaics along the kerb,

spandrels of gold between car wheels. Werewolves,
gorgons, are sauntering out of their lairs, trick-or-treaters

with quince-red cheeks and my beautiful girl in a tent
of yellow roses twines her corn snake round her wrist.

As a night fox trots through a gold-barred gate, trapping
gold-dust in his fleece – quick, hammer him into the frieze.

In Search of the Animals

It's not that I went in search of the animals
though occasionally one crossed my path

or stole out of Wikipedia as if it were a wood
in an English shire but looking, for example,

at a daylight moon steadfast behind drifts
of cloud I'd follow my own drift of thought

and who's to say I wouldn't trip up –
moon not moon at all but a platinum sun,

a frieze of haunches, heads, ears and mouths
evening out, dissolving back to cloud?

And look how morning becomes evening
accidentally, heuristically, in the miracle

of language leading us up the garden path
a white rabbit crosses, a badger, our local fox

who is the last commuter padding home
apart from me, lagging behind on a crutch.

Martina's Radiance

Martina – you are in the mist now, season of mists
and mellow fruitfulness and indeed the apple tree

below my window holds reddening apples up to me
and Jude's apple tree has dropped enough fruit

for another round of *apfelstrudel*. Today the weather
suits you, dear Martina – sun's glow behind the mist,

raindrops I first mistook for petals on the pavement.
And isn't this what radiance is: the elation, the promise

before sun breaks through, the laugh behind your smile,
answers to questions you withheld – not unkindly or coyly

but because radiance and the soft veiling it demands
was your natural element? The new banisters I had built

will never feel your tread. But I feel it the way I feel
the air – more scent than air. Where would you have gone

with your stick, your crutch, had you been well today?
Where does mist go? Mist clears, Martina, clears.

Mehregan

She lifts the hood of the pram, attaches
a Chinesey floral scarf to the rim to cover

the opening behind which a baby sleeps
as the poem sleeps behind the page.

Wind lifts one corner. There's no heat
to speak of and the wind is only the earth

stirring as the year turns. But she covers him
as children do a table, making a house for him,

a darkened cave. What will he see but sprays,
borders thinned against the light, a chink

let in on his left? He has no left or right,
no borders, no China. Only this half-light,

the colour of his eyes, a colour bound to change.
Tomorrow is the autumn equinox, Mehregan,

a festival in honour of the Goddess Mehr
for whom my poem has been wheeled away.

Sun in the Window

Sun has propped her bike against the skyline.
She'll write in gold today. Wear pinks and reds,

wrap up warm and enter always smiling, always
ready to be overlooked, leaning her chin on her hands,

frowning when addressed. And as for desire,
she'll reserve it for praise, be it modest as an oculus,

a round open fenestration in a wall, set high
and facing west. Terraced, she'll rest her fingertips

on wooden muntins, angle her glance through windows
splayed in Polebrook or Threekingham. And how

she loves lancets, three trefoil-headed lancets, stepped!
A quiet soul she is, an altar rail around her thoughts,

the silk cordon hooked back on its brass stave.
And shy. But look at what she writes! Outshines

the others, the noisy, vociferous others, any day.
I'd give anything for a glyph from the star nib of her pen.

Bringing Down the Stars

As a mouse sniffs for cheese, so I, reading novels,
am sniffing out scintillas. Sometimes they are few

but enough to keep me going; at other times, rare
and completely enchanting, whole pages, paragraphs,

bring starlight down to earth. Over these I dither,
snuffle back and forth, inhale, raise my nose to weather,

glue it down to sniff the spark, to take the hit again.
I am on the trail of genius whose albedo is nothing short

of fallen snow's, desert sand's, who brings me the sky
'dove-gray with stars', 'the diamond lights of Yalta'.

So what difference does it make, under such reflectivity
diffused through time and space, if I'm here at Seven Dials

where the sundial pillar boasts only six blue clock dials
since it counts itself as the seventh or here on Upper Street

where blue battery lights twine round London planes,
each trunk a princely stag, each branch a starry antler?

The Cloud Sarcophagus

When I looked up, I was astonished at the muscularity
of clouds that were rearing up from a marble frieze

in high relief on a sarcophagus of blue. But whose?
Alexander's routing the Persians? Or Abdalonymus

the gardener king's, crowned by his very conqueror?
Now they revolved from war to peace and back again –

either way their spears were drawn, warriors, huntsmen,
lions snarling as they went, bundling up their hind legs

as if melting were a kind of leaping in slow motion.
And the cubs that littered their wake, play-fighting,

pouncing, rolling on their backs, were melting too,
panting, paws outstretched. What is to melt?

Into love, into war? Limb by limb to deliquesce,
to reaccumulate into a giant maw that swallows

a sun, a planet, like a ball in a baseball mitt,
a perfect fit, while the jaw, the hand, fragment?

The Doe

For however long it was – it seemed an age – that I stood
leaning over the wall, looking down on the sward below,

edging closer, I couldn't discern the slightest movement.
Only the wind that moved an ear like a stalk of wheat,

a jowl that quivered. Her eyes seemed not to see. The grass,
though abundant and inches from her lips, held no temptation.

Measuring her in perspective, as a painter with a pencil,
I judged her the length of my palm, on the thin side and brown,

a perfectly ordinary rabbit but for her stillness, her patience.
Finally, her trance broken, she jerked her head up, came to life,

listened, heard and bounded off with her white scut into cover.
I couldn't help but think of my mother – that same stillness,

that same absence of intention, volition, as she lay dying;
that surrendering of a life force that turns you to stone

though the fur is fur, the hair still hair, the posture neither
sleeping nor prone but poised on the cusp of sculpture.

Abney Park Cemetery

The air in the cemetery's greener, thicker with scent.
Paths wind and twist and, whenever I come this way,

I wonder if I've lost my bearings, following tiger stripes
of sun between the graves. But here's the station café.

A patient I know from the psychiatric ward waves,
smiling his dimpled, toothless smile, rubbing his forehead.

His voice, high-pitched, accented, carries even though
he's talking to a woman at his table. I'm fond of him –

he inspires affection. The skin around his eyes, wrinkled,
rayed, has the softness of my father's. He asks after Tom,

shows me the heel of his palm badly burned from the cooker.
'It's my mind that does this – God save me from accidents!'

He knows some Iranians, Azeris, just round the corner
at the snooker club. Whenever he goes in for a drink,

a Coca-Cola – and here he gestures, shrugging, meaning
it's on the house – 'it's', as Hassan says, 'hospitable.'

Migration

When I see a hand first raised, then placed
on the heart, the head tilted towards the heart,

a greeting exchanged between a pedestrian
and a passing bus driver; when I see a woman

seated at a bus stop wave to a woman passenger
sitting behind me and, picturing them still,

look straight into trees, tears spring to my eyes
even though we're stopped at Elephant & Castle.

All one way blows the wind in the trees but
which is the way to a staging post between

the Khalvatis now, scattered in the diaspora,
and our very first forebears who struck camp,

loaded their beasts, set their caravans against
a skyline, wind whipping the horses' manes,

the fringes of their saddlecloths and shawls,
and moved as a whole tribe together?

Her Anniversary

It might be grey, it might be cold, who knows
what the weather's like out there? Birds know,

so silent in the branches, animals in their lairs.
But I, my blinds drawn down, am blind to all

but my heart's November, the second anniversary
of my mother's death. Perhaps I can keep her in,

in the warmth of my rooms, fug of my flat rehung
with her paintings, her tapestried cushions strewn

on chairs and sofas, making them gardens, rosebeds.
I can sit there among them as she did, as we did,

oftentimes together. But where's the sense in that?
Their velvet backs, rusts and fawns she kept face up

to stop the flowers fading, are already grimed from
propping my back, my head. I can become her instead.

Willingly become her in every meaning of the word.
Daughters who betray mothers are in turn betrayed.

VI The Avenue

Granadilla de Abona I

Even this garden, a veritable Eden with a keyhole pool,
a white cockatoo glimpsed behind the bars of a cage,

a trailing orange lotus swaying shadows against a wall
and sun beginning to cast its warmth on rattan chairs,

is an orchard of sorts but with nothing wild about it
or left to chance, the body without the soul of an orchard.

An orchard's soul should be ragged, ramshackle, dapple
throwing honeycombs of shade on soil, weather interstitial.

But every view's an artwork. Trees laden with oranges
like Christmas trees with glass baubles, paired parakeets

as yellow and green as the orange trees, banana palms
sculptural, fronds sheared and scored, *cardones*, Magritte-like

– not cacti but as penile – black avocados in the background,
arbours within arbours, round every path another, offer

a series of small warm breaths: seclusion without solitude,
arrival without homecoming, a silence that rings in the ears.

Granadilla de Abona II

We are illicit. We creep around shaded paths, spit pips
into flowering shrubs at the root, leave wet handprints

on poolside tiles where we crouch to rinse our fingers,
talk in the most inaudible of murmurs. A scruffy old hen

crows triumphantly as she lays, a great tit flits into view
and, on being glimpsed, scares; we are here and welcome

only if we whisper without voice, move without noise,
leave pipettes of blossom to float by on stagnant currents.

Even our thoughts intrude, being the wiliest of burglars.
Sleep too is a violation or so the parrots would have you think,

screeching warnings enough to wake the dead. Don't breathe,
don't listen, walk if you can on air. Every path is a dead end.

Under the arch, the wrought-iron gates are not only padlocked
but so entangled with lotus – an explosion of orange fireworks –

they seem locked in perpetuity while, passing in a street, blaring
through loudspeakers, gospel singers belt out 'Oh Happy Day…'

Granadilla de Abona III

Well, no wonder. This is the site of the Garden of the Hesperides.
These the Islands of the Blessed, the Fortunate Isles where,

Sertorius waxed, 'the air was never extreme, which for rain
had a little silver dew, which of itself and without labour,

bore all pleasant fruit to their happy dwellers.' Pleasant fruit
was had in plenty – reach up and twist the golden apple

which will drop into your hand, the banana from its own hand,
the *madroño* from its cluster. Oranges will rain down like

starlight through a telescope, a green and golden galaxy.
Near enough to spy cobwebs between their nodes, leaves,

drained of their sap, crack and burn at the tip – the more
brittle they grow, the weightier grow the oranges. By their song,

imagine the size of canaries, goldcrests, lovebirds, lorikeets,
their invisible throats and beaks smaller than pumpkin seeds.

The length of life remaining to be lived can feel infinitesimal
and interminable too. Not every poet longs for immortality.

Granadilla de Abona IV

Periquito and I have the garden to ourselves.
Periquito has the shade and I the rising sun,

fierce as Periquito's fierce. 'Dominion' as in
'Multiply and have dominion over all the creatures

of the earth' has, in Hebrew, another meaning:
'understanding'. But Periquito talks Canarian,

a parrot dialect thereof which, all ears though I am,
signifies nothing but sound and fury. Periquito

has the aviary birds to chorus him. They twitter
like background water, he on one end and I

on the other of a diagonal across the morning.
Released from his cage he teeters along a parapet,

a white quiff, a waddle and limp. Nothing to say
for himself now that he's free. Later they'll call,

'*Periquito, hola hola*' and '*Hola*' he'll answer
as clearly as a boy, albino, hiding in the bushes.

Granadilla de Abona V

He whistles once, crosses from one citrus tree
to another along a hammock bridge, raises his quiff,

tests a twig with his beak, one foot held quivering.
In a sleek white tailcoat, his dress shirt ruffled,

he skids up a rope, waving a hand, claws curled,
attentive as a child in a playpen to the movements

of all and sundry. *Diario de Avisos*, freshly laid,
collects his droppings. Lord of the green canopy,

he swings below the hammock ties, perches in a cleft
to peer towards the sound of a generator whirring,

taps his left hand on the branch excitedly and twice
raises two white wings, once to declare himself an angel

and once for balance as he grows ever more excited,
hanging by his beak alone, doing chin-ups, sipping water,

shaking diamonds in a spray around him, at the approach
of Señora coming and going about her daily bustlings.

Granadilla de Abona VI

Here they come, the insects, feasting off the money plant
under the drago tree whose bloodsap and attendant cures

gave the Guanches health and longevity. My mother was
ninety-two when she died, last and oldest of three siblings.

Her family history died with her, none of it lives in my
or my children's memory. We are yesterday's people,

provisional, adaptable, borrowing and assimilating.
The Guanches were said to have been exiled by Trajan

whose captains cut off their tongues, put them in ships
laden with animals and seed and forcibly settled them

in the Canaries. Silbo Gomero, their whistling language,
has survived to this day along with municipal place names,

gofio, their staple bread, and mummies – light as scrolls
with skin thinner and softer than our best kid gloves –

that lined their burial caves. But the Guanche themselves,
decimated, enslaved, were erased from memory and texts.

Granadilla de Abona VII

On three dry pumpkins, some little white pebbles,
timples, a very small drago tambourine, a blonde flute

with a hollow reed and four pipes with green stems
and knobbly joints of barley, how sweetly they played

endechas: 'What does it matter if they take and bring
milk, water and bread, if Agarfa will not look at me?'

And while they played and sang songs of love and death,
the old Gomera people, bearers of wisdom and knowledge,

who kept their mysteries to themselves and never divulged
the sacred site of their necropolis, the mysterious words

pronounced when sowing seed or how their ancestors,
the indigenous people of these islands, came to be here,

saying only that a higher being had brought them, left them,
then wiped them from memory, while the old native songs

played on, the elders wept and rocked, leaning on their sticks
with the same, same veined hands as the mummy of Madrid's.

Plaza de los Remedios

It's the childlike geometry of the square –
the octagonal bandstand in the centre, the ring

of café tables and chairs around it, the outer ring
of bifurcating trunks, their packed suitcases of leaves,

benches, balconies, windows that ask to be counted –
that calls to mind set squares, rulers, compasses

and a head bent over a see-through protractor,
an angle of time arrested in the impalpable air.

The scene is as mild as a nativity and beyond this
simple geometry, immense, immeasurable mountains,

a stormy Atlantic you can hear at night, snoring
like a sleeping leviathan. I would like a small life.

I would like a son who takes both my hands in his
and, walking backwards, inches me towards the end

of a cobbled street where a door opens and a daughter,
taking my hands from his, helps me over the doorstep.

The Wheelhouse

Sun sinks behind the massif before it blazes, fires off
shadow through the balustrade. The square is a great ship

floating, rising and sinking on sun and shadow, a ship
in harbour. We stroll the decks, let wind rest in our sails.

But I know nothing of ships, wanting my feet on earth.
My mother's ashes under the cherry trees, her house

occupied by someone else. I never go there, just as she
will never sit in a café, holding her handbag close on her lap,

her scarf, her hair in place. Memory would fill her smile
as she swayed her head from side to side and breathed

sweet exhalations of regret. Peremptorily, she'd ask
for an ashtray, offer me cake. I loved forever being a child

at my mother's side, the captain of my ship whose railings
I peered over. All her absences are final now. Like wind

they've run in together. Now they form a wake; a house
I am more than welcome in, a wheel I must learn to steer.

Finca El Tejado

The juniper glistens with rain. Plumes, shadowed on the urn,
waver indistinctly. The fountain gushes, gushes, wind moans

and tugs at the palm fronds – join me, join me. Raindrops
hang two by two from railings. Everything has the shine

of black on it. Marina turns the music on and the room fills
with candlelight and yearning. Lamps throw umbrellas of light

against the walls, the red check tablecloth, a bottle of wine,
its candleglints, wait for company and we must stay with them,

listening to the fountain, gutters and the plucking of guitars
before the song begins. I have slung a quilt with violet roses

over the curtain rail to keep out the light in the morning.
Now I long for it, to see the sky, the golden stars of hamlets

high in the hills. I long to see the rain in massive drifts
open its fan, lay fan upon fan above the road to Buenavista

so that even the petrol station's blinded. Rose/leaf/rose/leaf
and through the open door a closed door, a shining lock and key.

The Avenue

I always knew my mother's funeral would be unseemly.
I never had the wherewithal. To have the wherewithal

is to inhabit a frame of mind that will stand one in stead.
In my dream a long avenue, pale with spindly poplars,

descended from the mountain – a peak like El Teide –
and along it walked on hind legs, but as naturally as men,

polar bears and among them my mother walked towards me.
Then I knew that all the separations I had suffered, all

the anguish they had caused me were but one separation,
one ball of anguish. And when I woke, I still could see

the avenue stretching to the mountains in mountain light,
the polar bears in file, solemn and steadily walking,

at intervals the silvery poplars on either side of the road
and in the middle my mother drawing slowly ever nearer

as if the avenue were a travelator moving in both directions,
carrying me forward towards her, carrying her forward towards me.

Ghazal: In Silence

Let them be, the battles you fought in silence.
Bury your shame, the worst you thought in silence.

At last my beloved has haggled with death.
'One more day' was the pearl she bought in silence.

At night she heard the blacksmith hammering chains,
at dawn the saw, the fretwork wrought in silence.

'The only wrong I've done is to live too long',
my beloved's eyes tell the court in silence.

The bell on her wrist was silent, her fingers
ice cold as the julep she brought in silence.

My beloved, under the shade of a palm,
was the girl, the mother I sought in silence.

'Mimijune! Mimijune!' My beloved's voice
climbs three steep notes for tears to thwart in silence.

Three syllables of equal weight, equal stress,
dropped in a well, keep falling short in silence.

Notes

I am indebted to the writers and artists on whose work I have drawn for some of the poems in this book.

'Marrakesh I–VI': this sequence draws on *Matisse in Morocco: The Paintings and Drawings 1912–1913*, exhibition catalogue (Washington: National Gallery of Art, 1990). The first part of 'Marrakesh IV' is a quotation from the catalogue essay 'The Moroccan Hinge' by guest curator Pierre Schneider. The second part of the poem is a quotation from Matisse himself, from a letter to Albert Marquet, also taken from *Matisse in Morocco*.

'Le Café Marocain': after the painting by Henri Matisse, 1912–13.

'Model for a Timeless Garden': after Olafur Oliasson's eponymous light installation exhibited at the *Light Show*, Hayward Gallery, 2013.

'The Soul Travels on Horseback': the poem draws on Juan Ramón Jiménez, *Platero and I*, translated by Salvador Ortiz-Carboneres (Coventry: Dangaroo Press, 1990).

'The Overmind': the poem draws on H.D.'s essay *Notes on Thought and Vision*, published together with *The Wise Sappho* (San Francisco: City Lights, 1982).

'Kusa-Hibari': the poem draws on and quotes from the essay of the same title by Lafcadio Hearn, published in *Kotto* (New York: Macmillan, 1910).

'On the Occasion of his 150th Anniversary': the phrase 'spark of the Gods' is taken from Friedrich Schiller's 'Ode to Joy', 1785 ('Freude, schöner Götterfunken…').

'Bringing Down the Stars': the quoted phrases are from Vladimir Nabokov, *Glory* (New York: McGraw-Hill International, 1971).

'Granadilla I–VII': the sequence draws on J.P. Camacho, *Guanches* (Puerto de la Cruz: Editorial Weston SL, 2012).